By Melissa Elder

NOSTALGIA

the mundane

NOSTALGIA

poems by

MELISSA ELDER

M&B BOOKS LLC

dedicated to
my girls

for bedtime stories.

For I'll follow my friend of the printed page

wherever he leads me on,

I'll follow him back to a vanished age,

and the joys of a life that's gone.

Edgar Guest

nos·tal·gia

[nəˈstaljə]

NOUN

a sentimental longing or wistful affection for the past, typically for a period or place with happy personal associations

POEMS

Rocks at Windows

Yes,
we were
the kids throwing rocks
at windows, calling them
down, sledding
at midnight, swimming
in hot springs, daring each other,
ourselves to kiss, streaking
with smiles, lost
in time, not knowing
our futures would
break us
all.

Sloppy Firsts

It wasn't cinematic,
lips moving gently toward each other,
hands running through hair,
butterflies,
an orchestral score sweeping over the scene,
only shock, terror,
eyes wide open,
and a deluge of spit to wipe off.

The Tracks

We didn't intentionally
step closer to death
white knuckling the railing
as it roared past,

we wanted the train
to drown our screams,
shutting our eyes
against all that was
out of our control,

hoping the train
would take them with it.

Jousting

I found confidence
saying hello
to someone new
in the hall.

It battled
the insecurity
in me when
they didn't say it back.

Teenage Trials

Another CD case stolen.
Another reason not to go on.

Gesundheit

We sat on her bed
whispering
about her first orgasm.
What was it like?
You know when you have
a really good sneeze?

I sat wondering all the ways
I could make myself sneeze.

I Hope

Will I ever again
experience the freedom
I did at midnight
at seventeen running
down a grassy hill
naked
my best friends next to me
laughing
uncontrollably?

Leg Gaps

After practice I stared in wonder at her perfect legs in the mirror. You know you have perfect legs, she said, if there are three gaps when you put your legs together, one at the ankle, one at the knees, and between your thighs, pointing to each. I put my legs together and looked down. No gaps. No gaps, I said, hoping to hide my embarrassment with a shrug. She looked. At least they're shaved, she said.

Outdated

He took me to the peak. I thought he would throw me off. He talked about his childhood. I waited for him to confess his sins. He laid a blanket when, tired of standing, I was convinced he would take hold of me. He just wanted to enjoy the view, unfortunately.

Running Away

The thought of him leaving
forced me outside
where I surrendered
to running,
knowing the wind
would hold me,
freedom
in birdsong,
the pavement
leading me
into the setting sun.

Missing You. Physically.

I felt my body shake
a starving kind of shake,
a different kind of ache,
shaking gaunt with hunger,
touching eyes I didn't know were wet,
shaking with pent up words,
craving relief shaking,
missing you. Physically. Shaking.

All Thumbs

He didn't mean to hurt me
when I put my heart,
so grateful to be held, in his hands.

He only knew to be a teenage boy.
And teenage boys are clumsy.

Small Kindnesses

Hearing someone
say his name,
I'm taken back
under the stars
my head on his arm
as he picks the
sharpest pieces
from my skin
reminding me
love still lives.

Madness

It's infuriating
how intoxicating
consuming
defining
I find
you.

Rope Swings

Hiking I stumbled
across
hanging from a tree
and above the water
a rope swing

that flew me
into laughing screams
over ponds, searches for
bridges, leaps from
cliffs into breath-stealing
lakes, tubing down unfamiliar
rivers, sprints into the deep
water of frozen oceans.

What happened to
my natural born abandon?

Life Preserver

They found me
drowning and pulled me
up, wrapped me
in laughs, fed me
confidence, and clothed me
in time.

Lunch: A+

His grades didn't say
he was very bright
or someone to copy from.
He didn't often attend math,
but at lunch
he soared above us
in conversation, making us
feel, for a minute,
the rest didn't matter.

Pay Attention

She spoke of AIDS and her wife,
privilege and hard times,
taught honesty and integrity,
graded us on participation.
I just thought she smelled nice.

Gossip

I wanted to talk
to her more than
I wanted to talk
about her.

Cut Short

After my friends told me he liked me
and I told his friends I liked him
we cut the loop
and met on the grass
next to the shaded tennis courts
and traded thoughts about-
mid-sentence he rested his head
on my leg while chewing a blade
of grass, an intimacy I'd never
read about.

Our Song

We both loved the song,
the shared harmony,
but the melody grew dull,
the chorus overplayed.

Seventeen

My friends crammed
into my parents' van,
laps the extra seats,
and we drove
to a remote spot,
the air mountain crisp.
Everyone had a job
to start the fire,
set up the camp chairs,
spread the blankets, candy.
Back in the van,
lined like sardines
there'd be
more laughing.

Teacher

I sat shamefully
while they laughed
at my bright pants,
only quieting
when the teacher said,
To be the most interesting person
in the room, you actually have to be
interesting. You're not interesting
if you're like everyone else.

Erase

I would chew
all my erasers
as a student
keeping in mind
nothing can be erased.

Educated

He was gay,
he said,
intelligence written
on his face,
speaking of a different
education, where
life teaches you
entirely to transform yourself for the comfort of your peers,
where vain hope was the teacher,
and desperation the criteria,
where hate whispers in the halls,
empathy is found in a different classroom,
and self-loathing holds the pencil.

Radio Static

Gravel,
wheat,
stars,

a rusted old truck
guiding us
to the darkest spot.

Not a soul,
not a sound,
not a flicker of light,

only us
and radio static
forbidding innocence fight.

Haunted

He was in my life
so brief a time,
forgotten before he left,

and yet he has a way
of lingering
in my dreams.

Both

I was
too young
to recognize
butterflies as signs of love
when his lips
first touched mine,

too old
to believe
that love could be
that easy.

Kitchen Sink Window

Pausing in the soapsuds,
a dish dripping in her hand,
leaning into the counter,
she stared at her
fields of yellow canola flowers
moving alongside the wind.

Frozen Alive

Where are we going?
I whispered, him
grabbing my hand.
The boys snuck us out.
It's a surprise,
he smiled.

The moon moving
on the water
below the bridge
the splash silenced
our falling screams,
freezing us
fully clothed
in that moment
when we jump—

Desperate Love

He was desperate
to love me
but more desperate
to change me.

Social Media

On stage
at the school
assembly I
did everything
in my power
to make them
laugh out loud,
to keep them
looking,
to get them
to like me,
to convince them
to love me.
I did
it all
to see
that thumbs up.

Borrowed

Borrowing
her clothes,
hoping to wear
her confidence
for the day.

Teacher

My favorite teacher,
his aged mugshot
on the news, arrested
for money fraud,
a comfort
he was
even now
still teaching.

Spanish Steps

The Spanish Steps buzzed with sound and light. La Scalinata di Trinità dei Monti on the corner of la Piazza di Spagna. We found refuge in doing nothing, listening to the water splash from la Fontana della Barcaccia. From his seat on the fountain's ledge, he licked the paper tenderly with the tip of his tongue. His fingers rolled the paper with the casualness and care of years of repetition. I smelled the tobacco from where I sat. Unlike the cigarettes of the neighbor breathing smoke back home, it was sweet. This gentleman spoke a slow soft Italian. *Assicurati di prendere le foglie.* Teaching his son the art of rolling his first cigarette.

Make It Count

Breathe in slowly.
Now out.
Okay,
what comes to mind? he asked.

You know when your back pops in the exact spot you didn't
know you needed? Hitting every green light. The sound of
crackling bread. Compliments from strangers. Birds eating from
your feeder. The book ending you hoped for. Jeans sliding on.
Handwritten recipes. The exact right poem.

Those are cute, he said, but I asked, what makes you
happy?

Good Old Days

Was it that easy,
life as a child,

or do I make it difficult,
my life right now?

Taking Christmas

We knew
we were poor.
Frayed hand-me-downs
sizes too big or too small.
What floods into me
from then is
their forgoing
what they'd
asked for
so we could
open something.

for Erma

One-hundred-four
and smart as a whip
I had to—
I thought—
ask her,

Erma,
do you ever regret
not getting married
and having children?

my cheeks burning
before she answered
slowly
in a cracked voice,
I never
wanted my wings clipped.

Her

Her timid smile taught me curiosity,
the scars on her arms empathy,
the abuse she experienced reality,
her mental illness sincerity,
her love for people charity,
and her gut-wrenching will to survive taught me
life is everything.

Drifting

When I find myself
alone, my mind, by default,
will drift to
the daily things
that weigh me down,

but if I'm really lucky,
my mind will drift
to Paris,

to the corner cafe
where the chairs faced out,
where we licked our cheeks
sticky with pastry,
and listened to high heels
on cobblestones, dreaming
of where people went,
an acoustic guitar
strumming our bones.

An Old Beauty

He didn't make a sound
while we brushed his hairs,
filling them with clips and bows,

his eyes closed,
his cheeks blushed,
a nice ruby red on his lips.

A quiet man
who only knew farming,
every day spent with cows.

His callused hands
folded in his lap
while we painted his eyebrows on.

We girls were
giddy to have
his time to ourselves.

Pride had left
while we did him up pretty,
but the grin on his lips was all him.

Grandma's Hands

As a little girl I noticed
the age spots on her hands.
As a teenager I noticed
the cow being milked at her hands.
As a new adult I noticed
the gentle kneading of her hands.
As a mother I notice
living in her delicate hands
a rare love.

Happy New Year

Out with the old,
in with the new.

Forgetting the old
built the new.

I Don't Remember

We filled our time sledding.
I don't remember cold.
We filled our time with bowls of buttery popcorn.
I don't remember calories.
We filled our time on long drives.
I don't remember gas money.
We filled our time on the couch talking.
I don't remember feeling unproductive.
I don't remember feeling a need for more.
We filled our time.

Dollhouse

Playing house
in the college dorm
galley kitchen,
pots and pans clanking, kissing
like grown-ups, fighting like
lovers, we knew so little
about what real felt like
talking about our future
like it belonged
to us.

Poetry on the Lips

I wrote a poem for you
I said, our faces turned
to the fire, feet resting
by the coals. Shaking,
I recited my anxious
feelings. He pulled me
into his chest, rested
his lips against my ear,
kissed it. Did he kiss
the part of me I aroused
in him? Aching for the shiver,
the earned kiss—
he doesn't remember
the poem—
I remember
what his lips heard.

Deja Entendu

He wants a divorce,
she said into the phone,
her sobs engraving
themselves in me.

Couldn't adulthood avoid
the words I said
when we were seventeen?
He doesn't know what he's giving up.

Mind Reader

She sat
bored in her decorated booth
and exaggerated head wrap.
She grabbed my hand,
tickling it,
talking about my past,
defining scenes from my childhood,
tracing my veins, whispering secrets,
speaking about my future.
I didn't hear a word, consumed
by her all knowing
my need to be tickled.

Songscapes

She took us
to the reservation
outside highway 78,
broad horizons, dirt roads and
dirt-hole toilets,
wild horses,
fry bread over a fire
while she taught us
the true names
of plants.
Dusk brought her father,
eyes closed,
quietly chanting
a songscape
for her coming home.

Guest

I met him when he was digging through our trash, his black teeth, his hung over posture, his hair matted from sleeping on hard surfaces for decades. I didn't consider our home lavish, but when he sat at our dining room table, the room looked embarrassing. He was kind, easy to converse with.

He had greater social grace and etiquette than most people I knew. I was twenty-five, he sixty. As he got ready to leave, fear spread through my limbs and crept into my voice. But how do you survive winters? It's easier to deal with the elements than people.

Individual

It takes one person
to lose hope in the future,
and one
to bring it back.

Hitchhiker

We found him
under the overpass
sitting on his bag,
a smell worse than any urine,
talking like he'd never seen
a human, a soft face.

Looking in the rearview
mirror, I wanted to pet him,
as the car closed in
around his sanity,
before we let him out.

Loving Parents

Having two loving parents
you grow up thinking
you're the best in the world.

Having children
you get
corrected quickly.

My Earliest Memory

I wore socks for gloves.
I was crying.
Pulling them off and holding
my fingers together, your hands
wrapped my skin entirely.
You shaped an oval
with your mouth and blew
hot relief into my fists.
It was bright, not from the sun
but the snow covering everything.

She was Home

She would ramble about her out of date clothes while fluffing
pillows. From the floor where she folded laundry, tell us she didn't
have anything to give. A wet rag in hand, mock her hair, the bags
under her eyes. She would giggle at her weight gain while closing
the oven and say, "They can cook better," when we ate the meal she
put on the table. Complaining about the furniture while tucking
us in, apologizing for the house never being clean.

Little Sister

Mistaking wasabi
for guacamole,
nose bleeds
from laughter,
entangling
the naked
Barbie dolls
secretly,
crying at
compliments,
wanting me
close,
this is why
I need you.

Solace

He didn't know I had driven to his house to break off our engagement. I coldly went back to the car as he cried. My parents waited by the door, ready to ask me how it went, breaking a person's heart. Between sobs I said, "I think he'll be all right."

I woke the next morning, not knowing when the crying had drifted into sleep. My dad was lying next to me, his arm draped over my shoulder—he must have snuck in—comforting the villain.

Chivalries of a younger brother

Laughing,
he mooned me.
My shock
sent me backwards
into a table,
falling to the floor.
He helped me up,
hugged me,
walked me
to my car-
talked of
hanging out
tomorrow.

No Words Necessary

It was raining
when my sister and I
walked through the door.
He was sitting on the floor
of our two-bedroom apartment
eating a bowl of noodles,
his smell giving him away.
He was watching cartoons
in the English he didn't speak.
My sister and I sat on the couch,
mom offering from the kitchen,
fruitlessly, he could sleep
in the only room left,
the 1982 station wagon.

Big Sister

You were
the first
to call me
funny,
no one doubting
your judgement,
cementing
my confidence
in your own,
inviting me
to sit with
your friends,
picking
my clothes,
this is why
I need you.

Let Her Sleep

There was a rhythm after school. I walked in, took off my backpack, tossed it against a wall, and then I found my mom to give today's list of needs, putting her to work. The other five did the same.

Today she was asleep on the couch. Her breasts, her body, her time, indentured to her children, someone who was once someone. The kind of peaceful sleep that comes from exhaustion, a body in constant motion inert on the couch.

Winter Mornings

I don't remember
dreading the frost
outside the comforter,
or the small halo
around the old lamp
in our house
that looked like
the middle of the night.
Maybe I remember
the warm smell
of the oatmeal
my mom stirred,
its gentle burn
down my throat
thawing me
inside out,
but I don't remember
my dad waking
before me,
running through the snow
in his pajamas
barefoot
to turn on the car
so by the time
I got in
the heat wrapped
around me.

Milk of the Poppy

My mom dipped the poppyseed
muffin first into butter,
then a bowl of sugar,
and our worries into oblivion.

Her Affairs

She explained
her affairs
through unrestrained tears,

the pain
behind each one,
how it was
out of her control,
how it wasn't
about Dad.

I wanted to hold her
the way she'd held us
and whisper, there, there,
it will be all right,
failing to mention
what mothers fail to mention,
the heart shattering
in my chest.

But Don't Forget

He found her,
he loved her
and, groveling,
he lost her.

Weeping,
he said goodbye to her
and before she turned around
he forgave her.

Stepmommy

It wasn't your fault,
the curt blaming,
the discomfort in groups,
the judgment,
the stares.

We were broken,
broken family,
personalities, lives.

Mending
only through
understanding.

Square Footage

Whatever the size
the house a child
grew up in
is the biggest
place on earth.

Old House

History speaks
in years
about generations
running the halls,
walls cracking,
I hear their calls
telling a story
about what the walls have seen,
polished floors
mothers cleaned,
clanking pots and pans,
hands and expressions worn
down, fathers' pipes,
children adored,
alive in the creeks
of the floorboards.

Unorthodox

The most exhilarating parts
never felt normal.
Hay bales are best for jumping,
trampolines for sleeping under the stars.
Midnight is the perfect time to swim.
I learned to drive in a snowstorm.
My first dance was in a barn.
A dare got me my first kiss.
I watched my mom give birth in her bedroom.

Go Fish

We share blood,
but mine needs
regular doses
of adrenaline
and hers does
better without.
Boating on rough water,
our uncle
reckless at the wheel,
the tube called to me
and chased her away.
I begged,
Come on,
you'll love it.
I was giddy
when I saw her
face cave before
she said it.
I scrunched next to her
on the tube to see
her smile up close.
Within minutes
she was sobbing.
Our uncle slowed
the boat for her
to gain her composure.
I was rolling my eyes

when from the water
she lifted a fish bone
speared through her big toe
the length of her middle finger.

Whistling

I didn't mind
walking home by myself
when the luxury of fear
hadn't been taught.

Exposed

The old man exposed himself to us, asked if we liked it. We turned and ran, legs and clenched fists pumping. Home and out of breath, squirming, we reported it to the neighbor kids and their laughs. Years after I couldn't look a man in the face knowing what was behind his zipper.

The squirming has faded, but my fists are still clenched.

Get on With It

Killing time,
shooting it
dead, burying it alive,
bashing my head,
doing everything I can
to speed it ahead,
doing everything I can
to kill it before bed.

When It's Quiet

What do you think about
when it's quiet,
the past, memories,
when the music's off,
your phone away,
when you're left
by yourself?
Who are you then?

Honeysuckle

Following the chirp and hum
of a hummingbird
we set our backpacks
against the vines
spilling onto the sidewalk
and sat down next to them,
and through missing teeth,
the tickles of soft leaves,
we giggled at each other,
and kissing
the velvety pedals to our lips
we drank the nectar drips.

Don't Wait

I wish
they were
kinder to me,
I whimpered.
Don't wait for kindness,
dear one.
Be kind.

Catch

I watched her bury
her son in the ground
and asked,
Where is God?

when I saw
behind her
hundreds waiting
to catch her.

Found

How can someone be lost
if they're home
to everyone else?

A Plea from the Living

We said silent goodbyes
to his grandfather
in the open casket,
moving down the line,
his cousin with Down syndrome
climbing into the wood bed
to open his sleeping eyes,
begging him
to wake up,
we dared to hope.

Hanging Eggs

Boredom sometimes inspires
an idea for a dozen eggs
filled with havoc
and angst. We threw
the eggs tied with string
over telephone wires
strung across the road
and waited. The first car
drove right past it,
the second straight into
the yoke drenching
the windshield. The car
swerved to the side of the road.
We heard the spit flying
obscenities before he opened
the door, yelling for the kids
who threw a direct hit. We
laughed from the water tower,
anxious not to be late for dinner.

Antsy

He arrived
at seven sharp—
a good sign.
While I put on my coat
he stood in the doorway
and stared
gape mouthed
at the living room carpet.
Mid sleeve I followed
his eyes,
a straight line
to a waffle,
an army
of ants.
Someone else
will clean that up,
I said.
Let's go,
I'm hungry too.

Married Young

No one told
us the fear future
gives. No divorce,
no affairs, no people
getting tired of
one another. Not
us! Eyes closed
to the ground
children would shake,
careers ruining lives. Ignorant
of student's loans
crushing weight,
even meeting
basic needs,
all the ways
it might unravel.
I just wanted
someone to talk to,
hold hands with.

No Turning Back

I've made up my mind.
No.
No more.
It's done,
finished.
It is what it is.
It's over.

I want you.

Poet

I smile
thinking of the writer
tapping His chin
pen in hand
Himself smiling
at the story,

At fifteen I held hands
with the boy who
became my husband.

Honeymoon

Marriage began
the second I walked in
on him naked
on the toilet,
reading a book, relaxed
as a man about to
light a pipe,
straightening the crease
on the page.

Body Shop

They talked
mechanics,
this goes here,
that there,
missing the best parts,
timidly touching new places,
blushed smiles
showing their innocence,
fear fueling passion,
kissing the range of skin,
forgetting cold pillows,
now a shared bed,
heated with breathing.

RX Oxymoron

Don't have kids
he said,
his eyes
on the notes
he was writing.
That will help
stop the spread
of type 1 diabetes.
His years of study
and dedication
filled the walls
with his accolades.

Sting

In a tone
angry
and derisive
I screamed
at my mom, my dad
running downstairs
before I finished
my— and, regretting it
to this day, slapped
my sixteen-year-old
mouth right on the lips,
a swollen sting I
feel every time
my child yells
at me.

Topsytail

"Mom, will you do my hair pretty today?
I want to look old."

She took me to the bathroom,
gently playing with my hair
before getting the brush wet.

She took her time,
pulling my hair tight,
flipping it right
down the middle for the prettiest topsytail
I've ever seen.

The Dig

I saw him digging
deep.
I couldn't look away
but then
he ate it
like he had always meant to.

It was the first time
I disliked someone
for something
so small.

Recess

I'll never forget the wind,
pumping my legs harder than
I ever had, aiming for
the height of the bar,
hands white knuckled around
the chain, reaching
my toes. There was a split
second, before the buckle,
when unbelievably
I believed I would take off
before the bell rang.

Hope

A certain calm
enters my mind
when I think
back
to childhood

an innocence
a stillness
a peace.

Girl on a Swing

I see you,
little blonde girl,
swinging under the tree alone,

pumping your legs
up to the sky,
why are you on your own?

No mom out searching,
no brother looking,
dad not calling your name,

passing the time
imagining places and things,
no one else playing your game,

singing as loud
as your lungs will allow
smiling ear to ear.

Happy to be
by yourself there
doing what you most hold dear,

unaware one day
your heart will ache
thinking about a swing

and a girl by herself
except for a song
that she sings.

Take Me Back

For one minute.
I'll make it brief.
I won't reminisce
or keep us too long.
I won't bring up what isn't.
Bear with me, sit in it
one minute,
a sliver (of time)
I'm claiming as mine.
Take me back
for one more minute.

Buried

They spied through a hole in the wall. Her two brothers on the other side of the wall, eyes glazed over, hunched over a 1960s *Playboy*. A sound in the kitchen broke their trance. Slapping the magazine shut, they tucked it under the mattress, secrets pushed beneath comfort, with the rest of the mess that accumulated there. She and her friend snuck into the bedroom. Holding the collection away from themselves as if it burned, they carried it up the hill. Finding a burial spot, they dug. Finally the hole was big enough for a shoe box. They put the magazines in it, and covering the breasts with dirt, buried them alive.

Where Justice, Love, and Mercy Meet

I had pushed too many buttons.
She pushed my desk against hers.
Kids laughed, made fun,
but I didn't goof off,
get distracted.
She walked me through
my math problems,
encouraged,
while, with a wink,
sliding Life Savers
across my desk.

Sexiest Braces Alive

At thirteen,
for the first time,
I had the thought
he's the sexiest person
I've ever seen,

sitting quietly,
not disturbing anyone
or showing off,
his braces,
his gelled hair
making his freckles pop.

Puberty's Recipe

Moody cramps,
zitty personality,
boobs in rebellion,
crushes in hysterics,
mess of hair, waking
blood,
and the body's sewers.

Exposed Insecurities

I egged him on,
making fun of
his hair, the weak arms
and skinny ankles
of his lurpy body,
taunting him with snowballs
until I saw it switch in his eyes
and, teeth grinding, he charged
at me, throwing my body to the ground
and smashing my face into the snow,
the laughter of the other kids
getting muffled. Suffocating
became real
until he grew tired finally
and, tasting blood,
I caught my breath.

Home by Six

We left
in the morning
without plan
or destination,
no way to text,
no way to know,
only faith
a stranger would give
us the time
so we'd be home
by six—a miracle
we ever ate dinner.

Daydream

A lighthouse in
the near distance,
small pebbles
instead of sand,

smooth boulders
for reading books,
wildflowers
to rest my head.

Endless trees
surround the rocks,
waves crash
on the shore,

I find seashells
near the driftwood,
moss blankets for
a forest floor,

a cool breeze
in the sunlight
where I lay
my patched quilt down.

Rocks skip
across the surf

and across
their ripples' sound.

Warm bread,
a glass of cider,
and from the
mussel basket steam,

in my limbs
and on my tongue
lives the escape
within my daydream.

Oma

Within her memories lay the torment of war. Boys' bodies hanging in the trees, the butcher's from the street lamp. Starving body and bone. Hidden in disguise from unrestrained soldiers. Cities, once called home now bombed and rubbled.

Here on the porch, face leaned into the sun, she sits smoking her cigarette, exhaling into the world. Smiling, while her grandchildren dance, for every second taking her further away.

Diverged

A contradiction
in a single person
two rights
truth taught
versus
truth observed
seldom aligned
both are me
but only one
can lead

I'll Let You Know

Are you
what you wanted to be
when you grew up?
the nineteen-year-old asked me.

With wrinkled eyes
I said,
I'll let you know when I grow up.

Can't Wait

As a little girl
I couldn't wait
to be twelve
shaving my legs
growing breasts
finally taken seriously,

at twelve
I couldn't wait
to date
always somewhere to go
driving
kissing
finally admired,

as a teenager
I couldn't wait
to be twenty-one
educated
eager to start
my own life
finally mature,

at twenty-one
I couldn't wait
to marry
companionship

mingled with travel
finally loved,

as a married woman
I couldn't wait
to have kids
holding babies
close to my chest
finally in love,

as a mother
I can't wait
to find myself again
reclaim what was shelved
finally rekindled.

I can't wait...

Nostalgia

When does
memory
take root
lingering
in limb
and loin
waiting
patiently
to be felt
again?

ACKNOWLEDGEMENTS

They say it takes one person to believe in you to believe in yourself. K.J. Wetherholt is my person. When I'll think back to this time in my life, I will always think of you, K. Thank you for believing in me, for publishing me, for editing me, and for the never-ending patience with me. Your kind strokes of encouragement made writing a book, I dare say, a pleasant one. Thank you, K.

Thank you to Anthony Garrett, my editor. You breathed life back into my writing and jumped on this wagon with me without blinking. You inspired me, taught me, and stretched me to a climbing potential. Your voice and wisdom permanently in my brain while I write. Thank you for taking your time and focus to do more than edit. Your friendship alone deserves a standing ovation.

To my friend turned family, Maria Hackett. It was years ago when I sent you my first poem while you were in Hong Kong, and you sent me your art. Now to have our work side by side in a book. Thank you for fulfilling this fantasy. I would have never done it without you. You are the reason people even glance at these books.

Ryan Elder, my brother, my friend, my go-to for all things design. Your eye for design and detail are impeccable. I'm so grateful for every second you spent perfecting this book with me. I'll never forget designing the cover with you and Scott into the late night at the cabin. Memories I'll cherish forever.

Thank you, Brad. My Brad. My muse. My love. The real poet.

Thank you, my dear girls. You sacrificed moments of your childhood with me so I could write about mine. I love you more than any part of my past.

Thank you to my parents. All of you. Mom, Dad, Laura, Lisa and Jeff. My village. You all supported me endlessly. Each one of you inspired poetry within this book, and each one of you inspired faith within myself.

Mom and Dad, I want to especially thank you for letting me write about personal and raw experiences. It's not easy to be so exposed. I'm so grateful for your gifts of vulnerability.

Thank you to every person who has entered my life, whether by chance or by choice. To every friend in every phase, every family member, every stranger, teacher, boyfriend, fling, acquaintance-you've taught me, shaped me and beautified my life. A life I'm proud to write about.

And thank you to you, kind reader. For spending your precious time reading my words. It's a type of magic I didn't know existed.

Melissa Elder lives on the east coast in Jersey with her husband and two girls amongst the trees. She loves the written word and enjoys writing words, too. She is the author of *The Mundane,* her first book of poetry published in 2022. *Nostalgia* is her second book.

www.ingramcontent.com/pod-product-compliance
Lightning Source LLC
Chambersburg PA
CBHW041328120726
48005CB00014B/2166